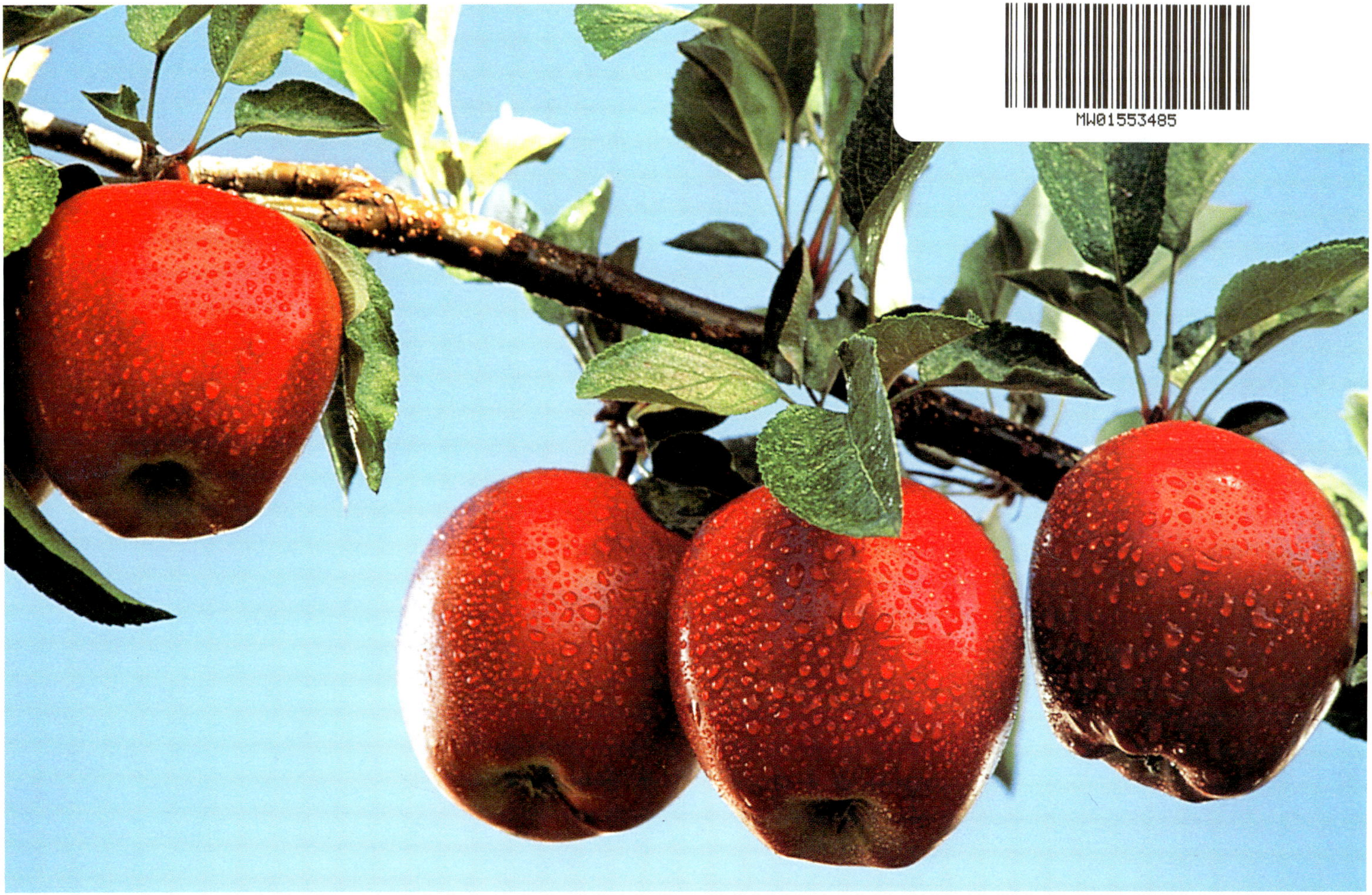

apples

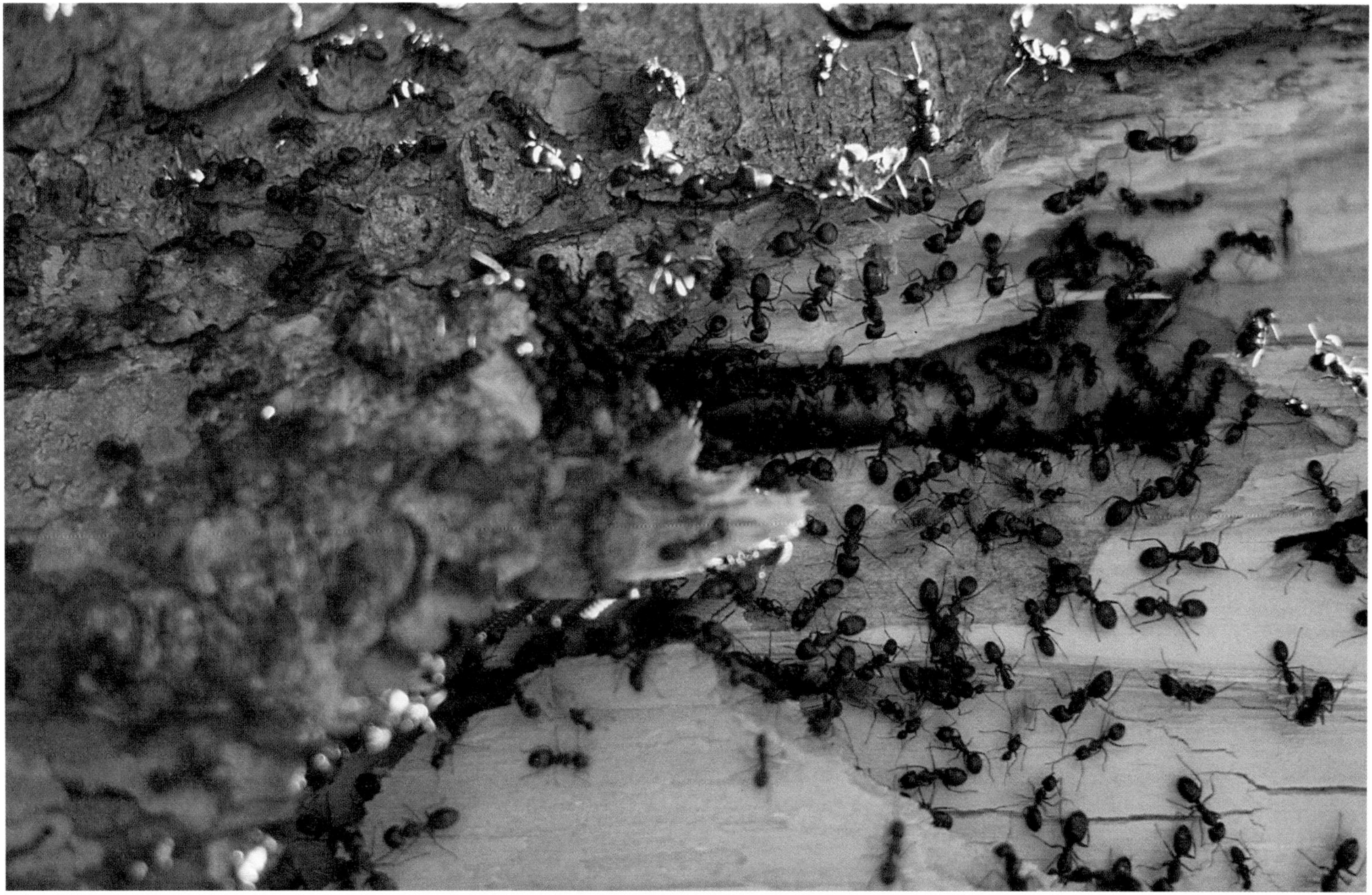

ants

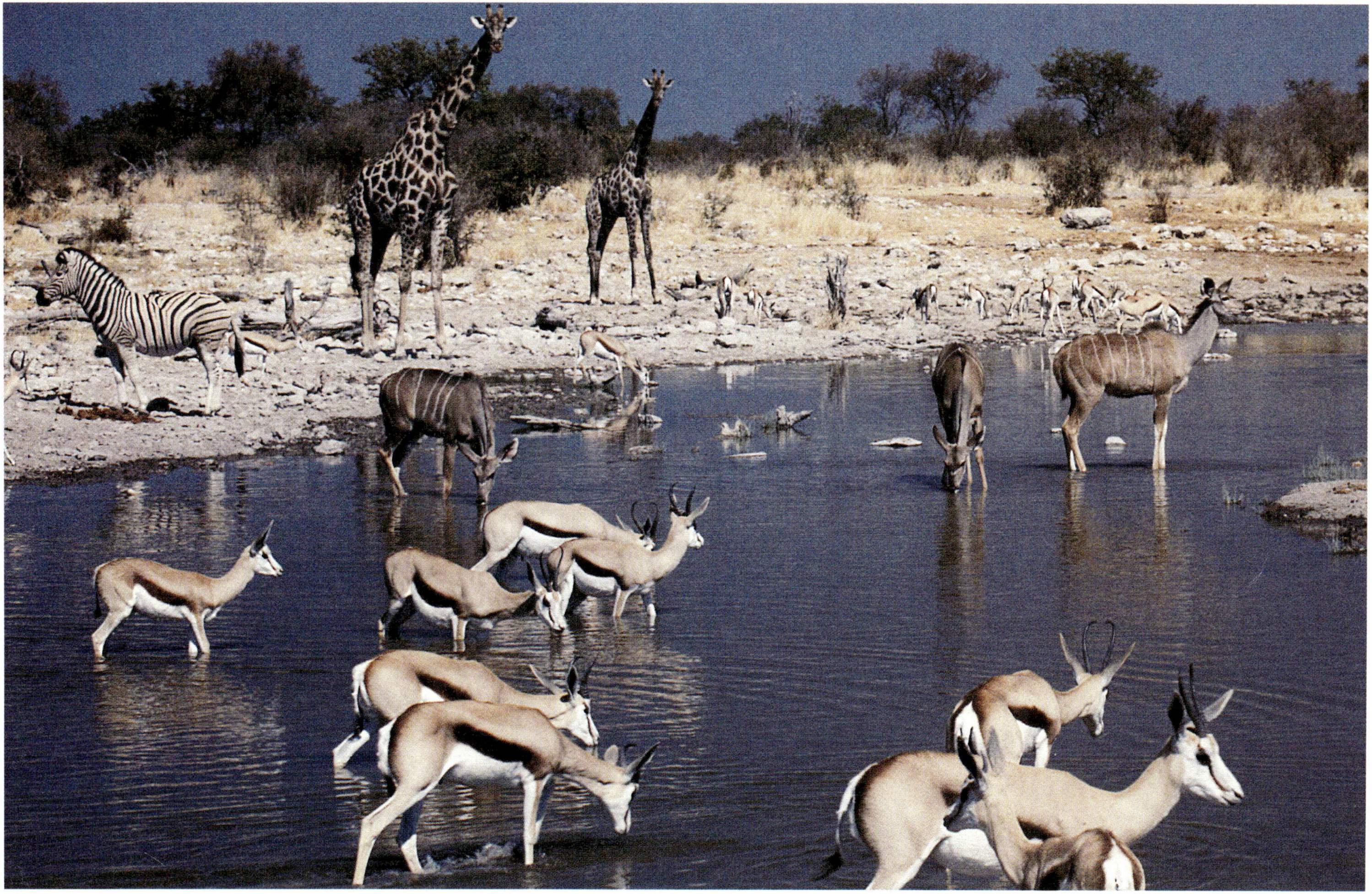

animals

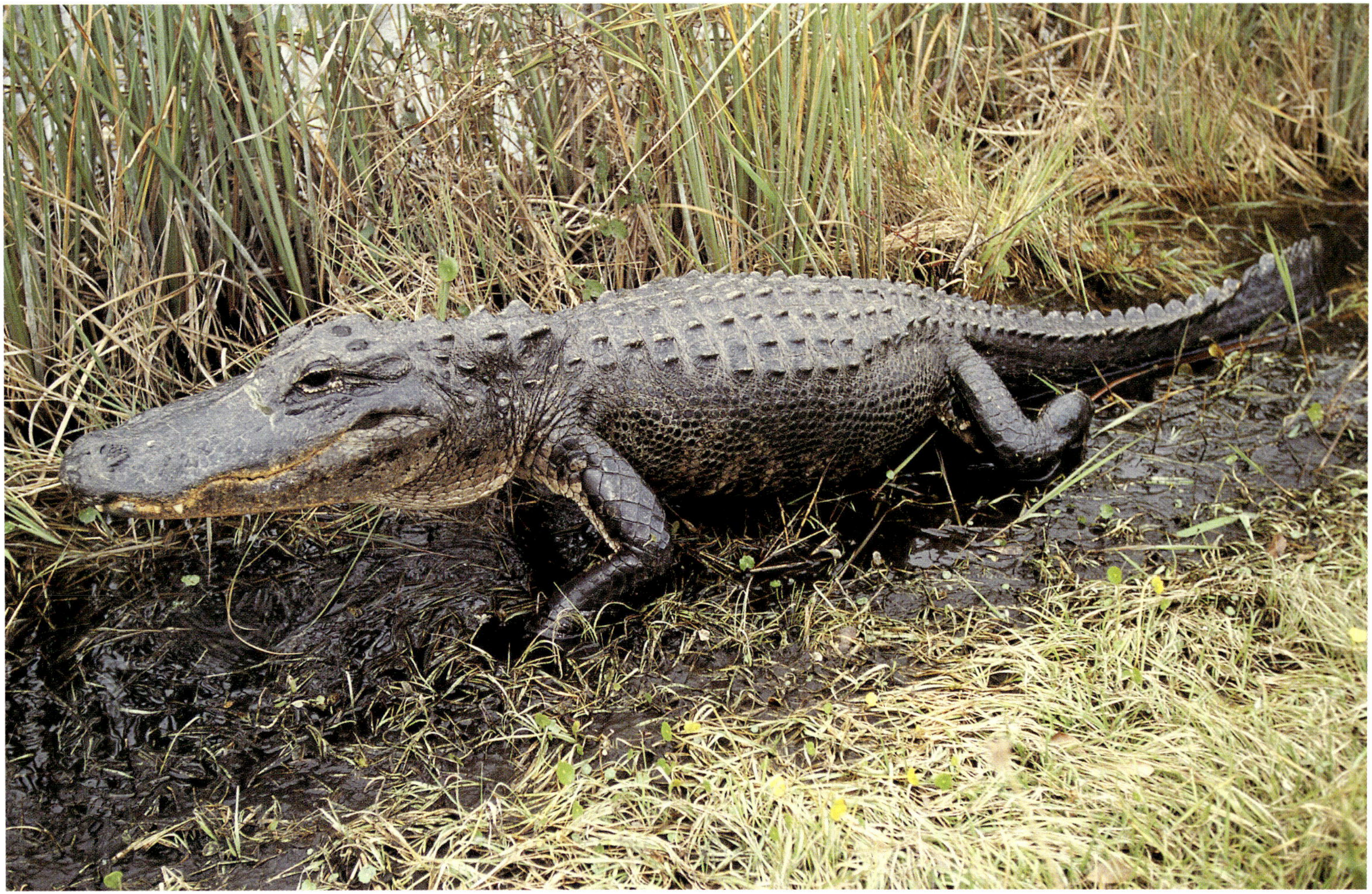

alligator

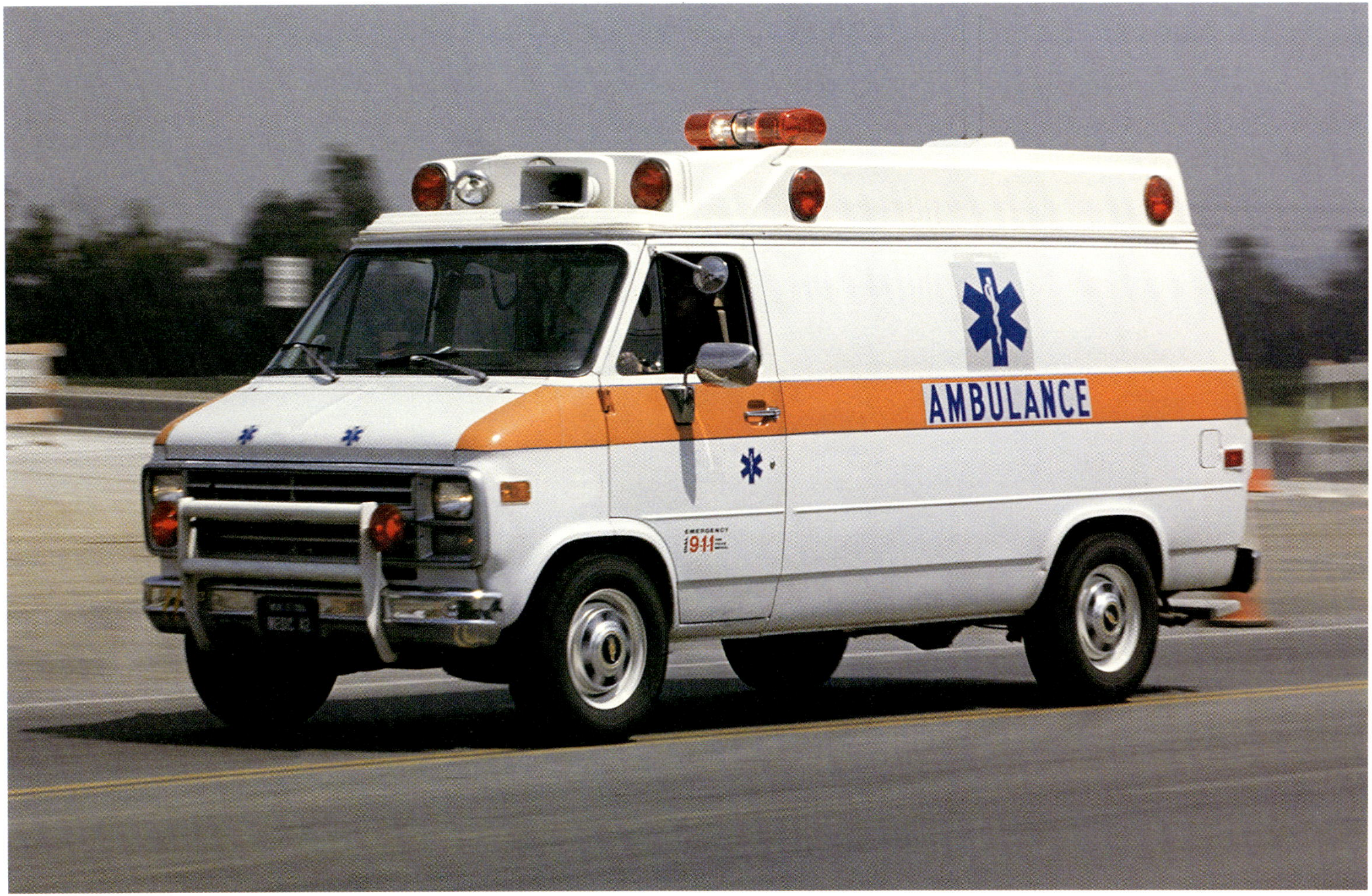
AMBULANCE
EMERGENCY
911

ambulance

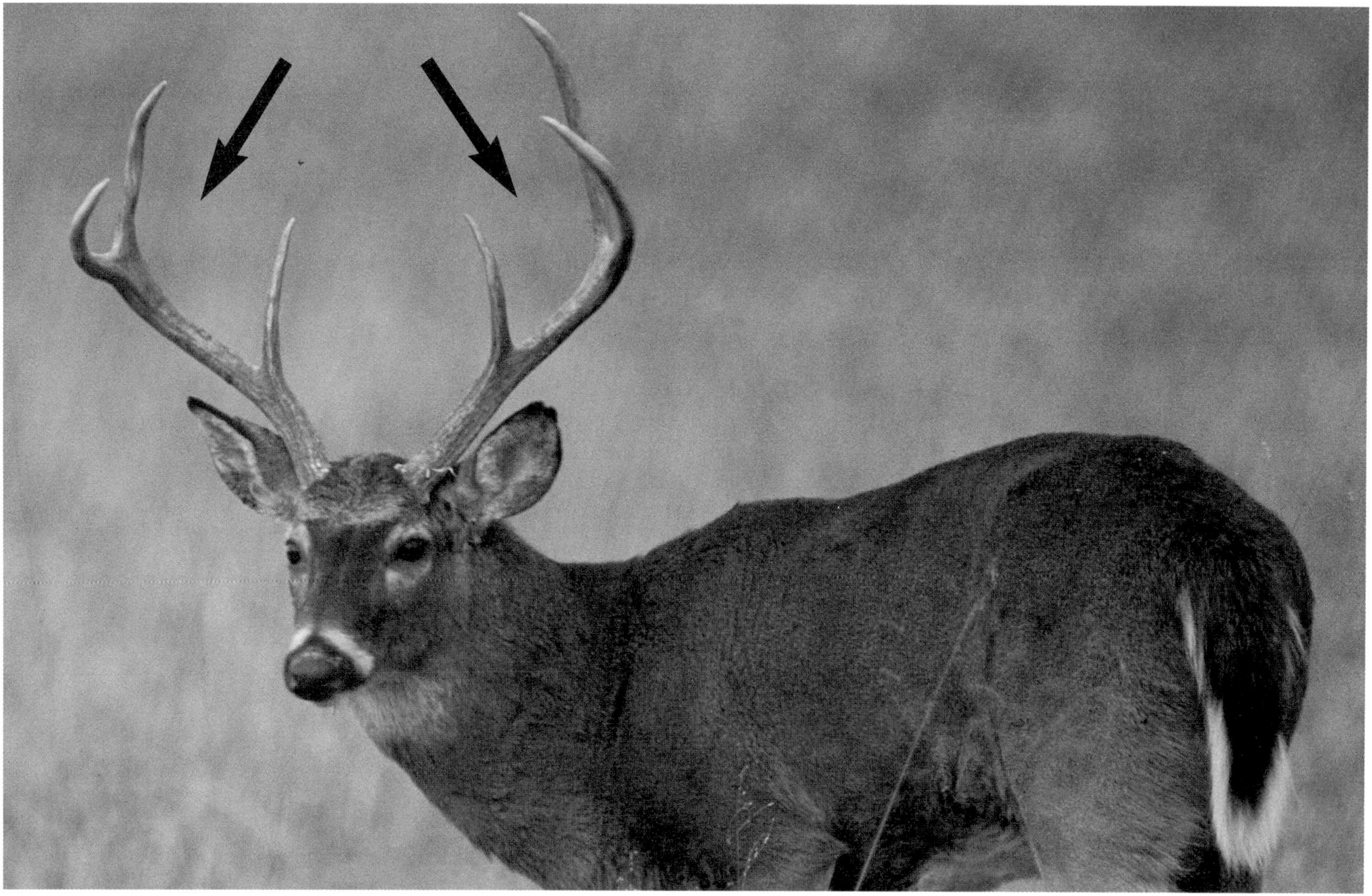

antlers

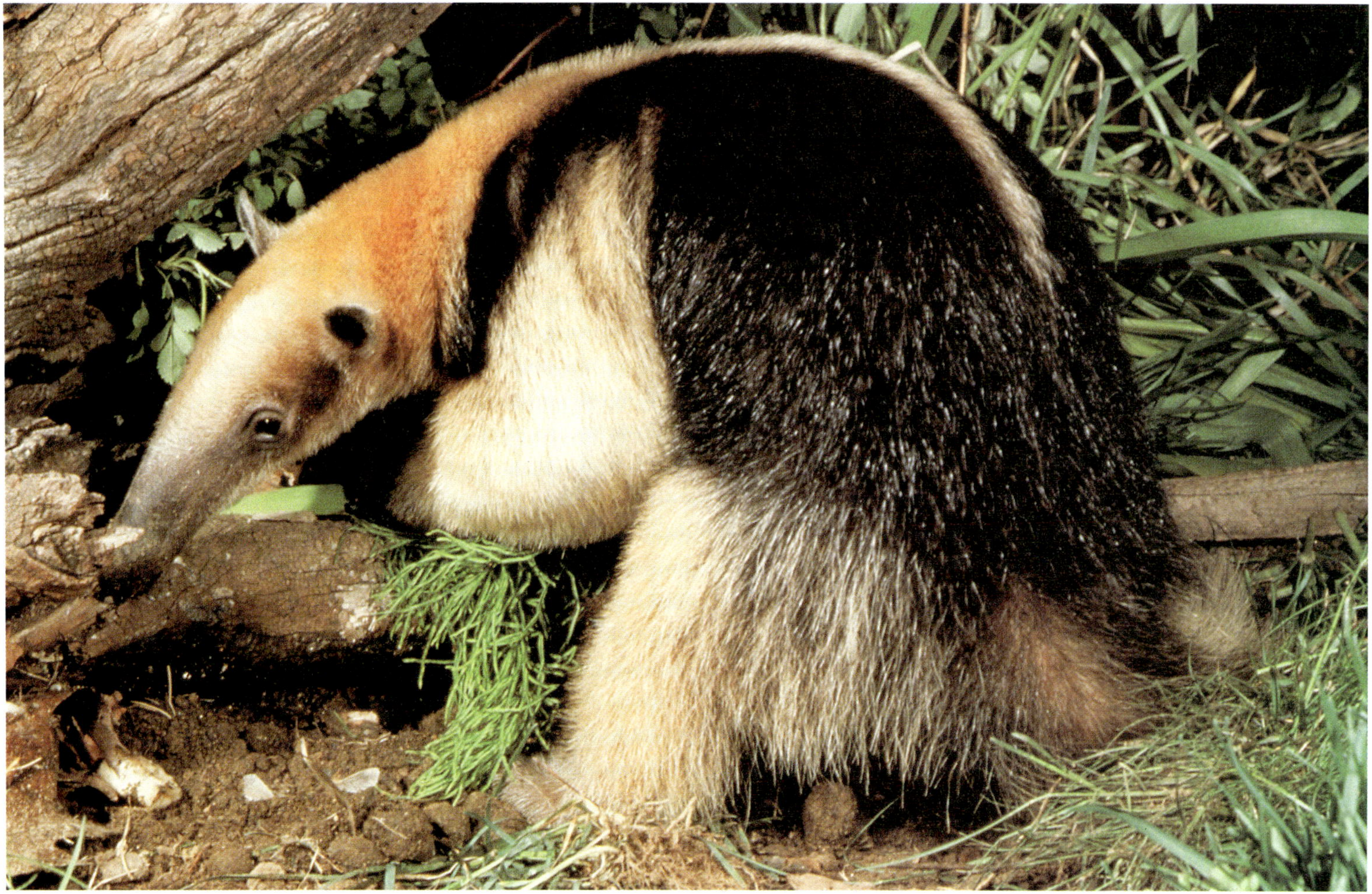

anteater

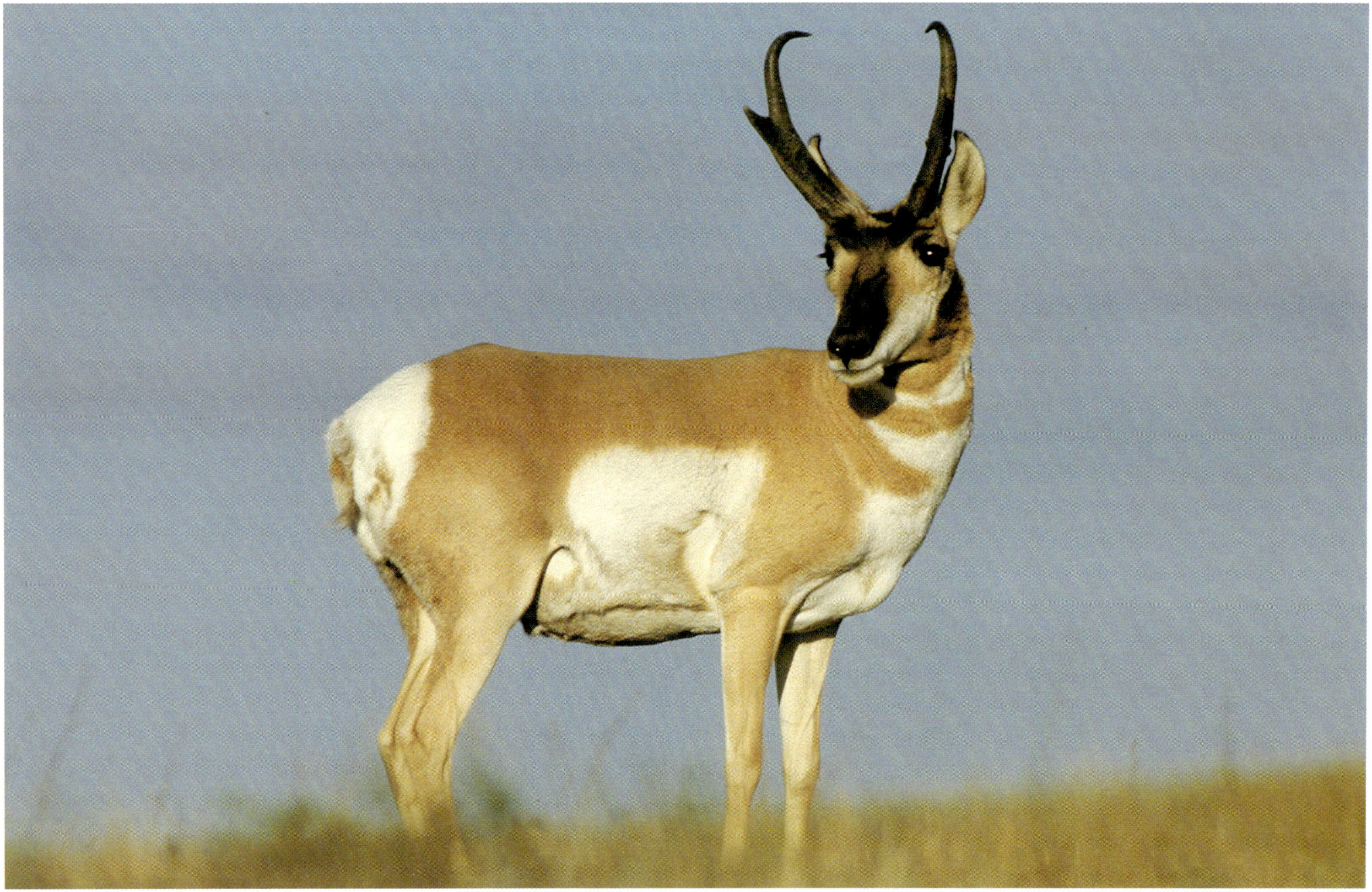

antelope